The Inca

Charles and Linda George

BLACKBIRCH PRESS

An imprint of Thomson Gale, a part of The Thomson Corporation

THOMSON
™
GALE

Detroit • New York • San Francisco • San Diego • New Haven, Conn. • Waterville, Maine • London • Munich

LIBRARY OF CONGRESS CATALOGING-IN-PUBLICATION DATA

George, Charles, 1949–
    The Inca / by Charles George and Linda George.
        p. cm. — (Life during the great civilizations)
    Includes bibliographical references and index.
    ISBN 1-4103-0529-5 (hardcover : alk. paper)
    1. Incas—History. 2. Incas—Social life and customs. I. George, Linda. II. Title. III. Series.

    F3429.G38 2005
    985'.01—dc22

                                                    2004021393

Printed in the United States
10 9 8 7 6 5 4 3 2 1

Contents

The Inca World

At the height of its power, the Inca empire of South America extended 2,500 miles (4,022km) north and south along the continent's western edge and between 100 and 350 miles (161 and 563km) inland. The Inca created this empire in less than one hundred years. From humble beginnings in the Andes Mountains of what is now Peru, the Inca conquered and ruled the largest native empire in the Western Hemisphere. Their success was short-lived, however. A few generations later, the conquerors became the conquered when Francisco Pizarro and his Spanish troops arrived in Peru in 1532.

Before the Spanish Conquest, the Inca empire included about 380,000 square miles (988,000 square kilometers), roughly the area of Texas and New Mexico combined. They called their empire Tahuantinsuyu, "Land of the Four Quarters." The empire included parts of modern-day Ecuador, Bolivia, Peru, Argentina, and Chile. On the Pacific coast of South America, the empire contained one of the most arid deserts on Earth. From there, it crossed snow-capped Andean mountains as high as 22,000 feet (6,705m), fertile mountain valleys, and eventually dropped into steamy tropical rain forests at the edge of the Amazon Basin.

Since the Inca never developed a written language, much of what we know about them comes from archaeological discoveries. However, a wealth of information about how the Inca lived comes from documents written by Spanish conquerors or Inca descendants during the Spanish colonial period.

*Opposite Page: The Incan ruins of Machu Picchu
sit atop the Andes in Peru. The Inca ruled the
largest native empire in the Western Hemisphere.*

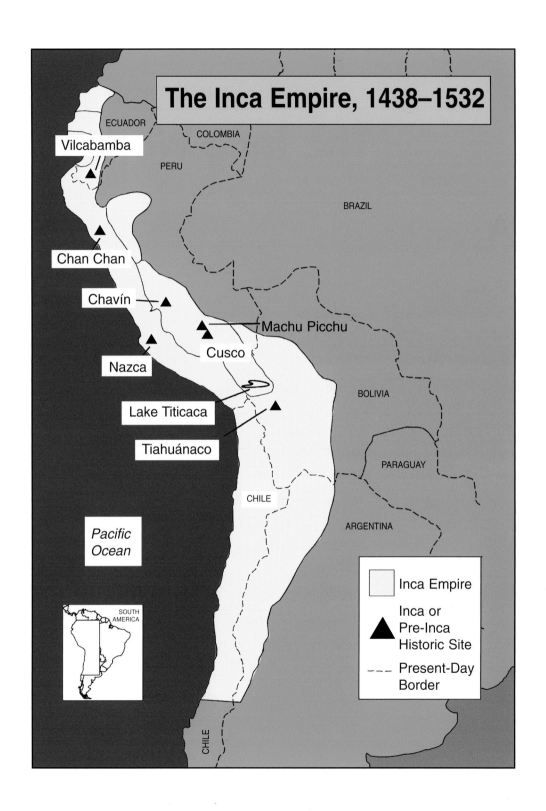

The Inca Empire, 1438–1532

ECUADOR

COLOMBIA

PERU

BRAZIL

Vilcabamba

Chan Chan

Chavín

Machu Picchu

Cusco

Nazca

BOLIVIA

Lake Titicaca

Tiahuánaco

PARAGUAY

CHILE

ARGENTINA

Pacific
Ocean

SOUTH
AMERICA

CHILE

Inca Empire

Inca or
Pre-Inca
Historic Site

Present-Day
Border

Unraveling the Mystery of the Inca

Firsthand information about the Inca comes from various sources. Pedro Cieza de León, a member of Pizarro's Spanish army, wrote *The Incas* about his experiences during and after the conquest. His account contains remarkable detail about the Inca empire.

Nueva Corónica y Buen Gobierno, an eleven-hundred-page letter from Peru native Felipe Guamán Poma de Ayala to the king of Spain, protests the treatment of Andean natives at the hands of the Spanish. It contains exceptional detail about Incan daily life and the history of the Inca before the conquest. It also includes four hundred drawings depicting Incan life.

The third written account comes from a Jesuit missionary, Father Bernabé Cobo. He was sent to the New World in the 1600s to convert its natives to Christianity and wrote *History of the New World, History of the Inca Empire*, and *Inca Religion and Customs*. Combined, these are considered by many to be the most complete history of the Inca empire.

Inca warriors (right) and laborers are shown in this 16th-century drawing. Firsthand information about the Inca comes from historical accounts.

Perhaps the most picturesque history of the Inca comes from "El Inca" Garcilaso de la Vega, born in Peru in 1535. His was a unique situation. He saw the Inca empire from two perspectives—that of its conquerors and that of a member of its society—because his father was a Spanish conquistador and his mother was the granddaughter of Huayna Capac, the eleventh Incan king. His seven-hundred-thousand-word chronicle, *Royal Commentaries of the Incas and General History of Peru*, relates legends of Inca origins as well as recollections of his childhood in Peru.

Que es la luz de las tinieblas ablu admirable luz.

MAYTA CAPAC INGA IV.

na El Melancolico Conquisto a los Charcas
s hasta el famoso Cerro de Potosi Hizo el ce
Co lebre Puente de Apurimac para sus con
La quistas Tuvo 50 Hijos Vivio 120 años
ello la Coya fue Mama Chimbo Ya chi Vrma
Sucediole su Hijo

CAPAC YVPANQVI INGA
El Avariento descubrio y el tesoro e
des riquezas Conquisto a los Ayma y
y Qtuchuas, y otras Provincias de la
rra, y Valles. Mando q se entierra
con sus joyas Vivio 140 años La C
Mama Chimbo Cahua sucediole su H

CHAPTER ONE

Incan Government and Society

Until A.D. 1438, the Inca were content to remain in the Cusco valley, in what is today Peru, and wage war against nearby tribes. In that year, a northern tribe, the Chancas, attacked their capital city, also called Cusco. Inca Yupanqui, son of the current Incan king, led the defense of the city and defeated the Chancas. Later, he claimed the throne and added to his name the word *pachacuti*, which means "he who transforms the earth."

Pachacuti, the founder of the Inca empire, lived up to his name. Over the following twenty-five years, he led his forces against enemies outside the Cusco valley and expanded his empire northward to near present-day Lima, Peru, and southward to Lake Titicaca. In 1463, he turned over leadership of the twenty-thousand-man Inca army to his son, Tupac Yupanqui.

While Tupac continued the empire's expansion, Pachacuti turned his attention to ruling his new territories and planning for the future. A brilliant civic planner, Pachacuti is credited with a city plan that transformed Cusco from a simple community to the seat of a vast empire. He designed and supervised the construction of many of its massive stone structures. He also established the efficient government and social organization that later characterized the Inca empire.

Opposite Page: Portraits of Cusco Incas are shown in this painting. The Inca stayed in the Cusco valley until 1438.

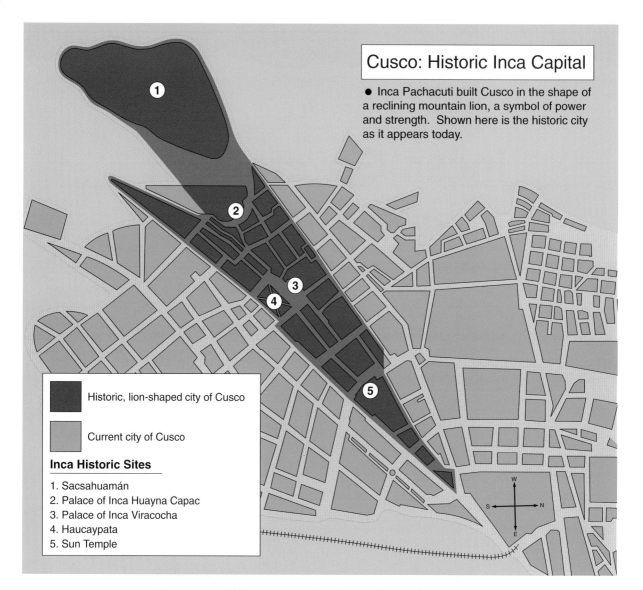

● Inca Pachacuti built Cusco in the shape of a reclining mountain lion, a symbol of power and strength. Shown here is the historic city as it appears today.

Historic, lion-shaped city of Cusco

Current city of Cusco

Inca Historic Sites

1. Sacsahuamán
2. Palace of Inca Huayna Capac
3. Palace of Inca Viracocha
4. Haucaypata
5. Sun Temple

Cusco: Heart of the Empire

Under Pachacuti's leadership, the capital city was laid out in the shape of a reclining mountain lion, symbol of power and strength. Near its heart is the central square, Haucaypata, the site of public assemblies and religious ceremonies.

At the lion's head, defending the city against outside invaders, lies a fortified temple complex called Sacsahuamán. This massive center boasts some of the Inca's finest stonework. Walls within this complex were constructed with thousands of stones, some as large as 13 feet (4m) high and weighing up to 100 tons (91MT). The Inca built these walls without mortar, and even today, the stones they carved fit so closely together that a knife blade cannot be inserted between them. Hiram Bingham, the explorer who discovered the lost Inca city of Machu Picchu in 1911, called Sacsahuamán "perhaps the most extraordinary structure built by ancient man in the Western Hemisphere. In fact, as an achievement of engineering, it stands without parallel in American antiquity."[1]

Cusco became the political, religious, and ceremonial center of the Incan world. At one time, it was the richest city in the Western Hemisphere, and perhaps in the world. From it, Pachacuti set up a highly centralized form of government and a rigid division of social classes, with the Inca emperor and his immediate family at the top of each.

An entrance of Sacsahuamán shows the close-fitting stone construction of the temple complex.

Inca Society

The Inca had a very rigid social structure. The emperor, whose title was Sapa Inca, and his wives, called *coyas*, had supreme control of the empire. The high priest and commander in chief of the army were next. Below them were the four regional rulers, the *apus*, and their regional army commanders.

Next came temple priests, architects, and administrators. Then came artisans, musicians, army captains, and the *quipuca-mayoc*, Inca accountants. At the bottom of the social ladder were farmers, herders, and laborers. Such a diverse and rigidly structured society required close supervision.

Land of the Four Quarters

Inca royalty honor the Sapa Inca in a 16th-century drawing.

Pachacuti knew that ruling a vast empire was not easy. In addition to having a large army, he had to develop sophisticated ways of organizing society. He knew, for example, that conquered peoples could be difficult to control without local supervision. For that reason, he organized his government so that local leaders made some decisions for their immediate areas, even though major decisions came from Cusco.

Chosen Women

Within Incan society was a special class called *acllyaconas*, or "chosen women." At around age ten, these young women were selected for their physical beauty and sent to schools to learn spinning, weaving, cooking, and other domestic duties. Those considered physically perfect were sacrificed to the Incan gods. Those who were not as perfect served as temple attendants or secondary wives of the Incan king. Some became *mamaconas*, or teachers of other chosen women.

One of the most important duties of the chosen women was the production of cloth. Another was the production of *chicha*, a cloudy fermented beer made primarily from corn. Although they had no personal freedom and were strictly controlled by the government, the chosen women were highly respected for their service to the empire.

He divided his empire into four sections, or quarters, roughly associated with directions from the heart of Cusco—northeast, northwest, southwest, and southeast.

Each quarter was ruled by an *apu* who answered to the emperor. These four *apus* were close advisers of the Sapa Inca. Each quarter was divided into provinces, and each province had a governor. In most cases, Pachacuti placed leaders from conquered groups in these positions, which allowed them to remain in power among their own people but required them to vow allegiance to the Sapa Inca. Each province was further divided into *ayllus*, or local communities, with local leaders. The *ayllus* varied in size, from small farming villages to larger towns. Every five years, an inspector—a *tucuyricoc*, meaning "he who sees all"—went to each *ayllu* to see how it was being run and to take a census of the population.

Pachacuti allowed conquered people to continue worshipping their own gods but maintained control by ordering that images of their gods be brought to Cusco to be housed in Inca temples. Because ancient people believed the images contained some of the power of their gods, this action was the same as the Sapa Inca holding his subjects' gods hostage.

A pre-Inca god adorns an ear ornament. The Incan emperor Pachacuti allowed conquered peoples to worship images of their own gods but kept the images in Inca temples.

Pachacuti also allowed the conquered peoples to speak their native languages but required them to learn the Inca language, Quechua. Finally, sons of conquered leaders were brought to Cusco to learn about the Inca way of life. While there, they, like the statues of the gods, served as hostages, which provided incentive for obedience among Incan subjects.

Inca Economy

After dealing with issues related to controlling his population, Pachacuti turned his attention to the empire's economy. The Inca empire did not have coined money, so taxation of the *ayllus* came in the form of work. Pachacuti required the head of each family to work a certain period of time each year for the empire, either in construction, farming, or in the army. This was called *m'ita* labor. Each person was assigned specific work for the empire depending on his or her skill—stonework, weaving, metalworking, and so forth. In return, the Sapa Inca provided food, clothing, and entertainment.

The economy was based on agriculture. Two-thirds of each farmer's crops went to the empire. Some was distributed to the general population, some was used for religious sacrifices, and some was given to the army. A large amount of the food was put into hundreds of government storehouses for emergencies such as droughts or wars.

The primary crops grown in the empire were white and sweet potatoes, maize (corn), quinoa (a variety of grain), beans, squash, tomatoes, chili peppers, avocados, and peanuts. Nonedible plants included cotton, gourds, and coca (for leaves that overcome fatigue when chewed). The Inca domesticated various animals, including llamas, alpacas, and dogs. They also raised ducks and guinea pigs for food.

Origin of the Children of the Sun

Scientists believe humans have lived in western South America for more than thirteen thousand years, first as hunter-gatherers, and later as farmers who formed small communities. Beginning about 1250 B.C., several advanced cultures developed in different parts of Peru. These cultures—the Chavín, Chimú, Nazca, Tiahuánaco, Huari, and Moche—developed skills in metalworking and masonry and built roads, irrigation systems, farming terraces, and cities that would later come under Incan control.

During the twelfth century A.D., a group living in the southern highlands of Peru, known today as the Inca, began to dominate neighboring kingdoms. They were one of many ethnic groups living in the Andes. No one knows what they called themselves at the time, because the term *Inca* did not come into use until much later. Around A.D. 1200, they migrated into the Cusco valley. Little is known of their early history other than the names of their leaders.

CHAPTER TWO

Daily Life

Information about the daily lives of common Incan people is scarce. More is known about the lifestyles, clothing, and possessions of Incan nobility, because more archaeological discoveries of Inca tombs have involved people of noble birth. However, a few documents, particularly those written by Garcilaso de la Vega and Gaumán Poma, offer insights into ordinary people's lives—what they wore, where they lived, what they ate, and how they celebrated the various stages of their lives.

What Did They Wear?

Incan men wore their hair short, in a distinct style to indicate to which *ayllu* they belonged. They wore a headband woven with special designs and possibly an emblem in the center of the forehead to indicate their social status. Only the Sapa Inca could wear a headband with fringe, usually red, or series of tassels hanging over the forehead. Incan women wore their hair long and never cut it unless in mourning or as a sign of disgrace.

An 18th-century illustration shows Inca nobles dressed in patterned clothing. Peasants wore plain clothing.

Inca Jewelry

Both Incan men and women wore jewelry. Most important for Incan noblemen were large earplugs, considered a sign of nobility. At an early age, the earlobes were pierced and a small disk inserted. As the person grew, smaller plugs were replaced with larger ones, until the lobes sometimes touched the person's shoulders. Most plugs had

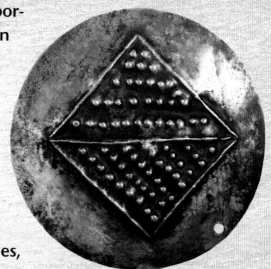

Metal discs like this were awarded to Inca warriors for bravery in war.

a diameter of about 2 inches (5cm) and were made of gold, silver, or seashell. Men also wore bracelets, and for bravery in war, soldiers were awarded metal disks that hung around their necks. Some wore necklaces of human teeth, taken from defeated enemies.

The basic clothing of the Inca varied according to their social status. Peasant men wore a simple sleeveless cotton or wool tunic, similar to a poncho, over a loincloth. Nobles wore the same type of garment, but made of finer cloth and with brightly colored patterns. Most Incan men also wore woolen or cotton fringes below their knees and around their ankles. In cold weather, they wore a cloak over their other garments. Incan women wore a large piece of cloth wrapped around their bodies, tied at the waist, and pinned at the shoulder. They wore another piece of cloth, similar to a shawl, over the shoulders and fastened in front with a large pin, or *tupu*. Both men and women wore simple sandals held to the feet with woolen straps.

A modern-day Peruvian woman carries her baby in a cloth like Inca women wore.

Incan emperors
wore an article
of clothing only
one time.

The Sapa Inca wore only the finest clothing made from finely woven cloth or animal skins often decorated with brightly colored feathers of tropical birds, even hummingbirds. One conquistador, observing an Incan emperor eating a meal, described the following:

> [One day] a slice of food was being lifted to his mouth when a drop fell onto the clothing he was wearing. . . . [He] rose and went into his chamber to change his dress and returned wearing a dark brown tunic and cloak . . . that was softer than silk. [I asked,] "Inca, of what is a robe as soft as this made?" He explained that it was from the skins of [vampire] bats that fly by night.[2]

Because Incan emperors were considered divine, clothing they had worn was also considered sacred. Each article of clothing was worn only once, then put into storage. Once a year, the emperor's clothing was burned in a special ceremony, its smoke becoming an offering to the gods.

Where Did They Live?

Incan homes, like the people's attire, varied according to the family's social status. Nobles lived in fine palaces, while common people lived in one-room adobe houses. The higher a person was in Incan society, the closer to the city he lived. The Sapa Inca and his family lived in the center of Cusco, while noble-men's families lived near the edges of the city. Peasants lived in the country, where they could raise the crops and livestock that would feed the nobility.

The typical Incan home was a rectangular building with a single room. It usually had one door, no windows, and a steeply sloping roof covered with thatch. In the center of the room stood a small clay oven. Few people possessed furniture, and all slept on the floor, even the Sapa Inca. In cities, structures were often grouped into a *cancha*, a compound of three or more buildings surrounding a central courtyard. In nice weather, the Inca used this court-yard for sharing meals.

An Incan home stands in the mountain mist. Social status determined where a family lived.

What Did They Eat?

The Inca ate two meals a day, one in the morning and one in the late afternoon. They ate sitting on the ground. Women sat with their backs to the men and faced their cooking pots. The Inca ate from flat plates and drank from tall wooden or pottery cups. Their favorite drink was *chicha*, a cloudy beer usually made from corn.

Incan women either boiled food in a pot or roasted it over an open flame. Most meals contained little meat. A typical meal might be corn kernels boiled with chili peppers and herbs, a soup made from guinea pig meat and thickened with potato flour, or cornmeal mixed with water and baked in hot ashes into a hard bread. It was not unusual for soups to be flavored with frogs, birds, or worms.

Some foods were preserved for storage and to make them easier to transport. Potatoes were freeze-dried in the dry mountain air. Corn was toasted so that it could be eaten while traveling. Meat was sometimes cut into thin strips, pounded, and then left to freeze overnight and dry in the hot midday sun. This meat was called *charqui*, which is the origin of the term "jerky."

Life Events

For the Inca, certain stages in a person's life were especially significant—a child's first haircut, puberty, marriage, and death. (Interestingly, a child's birth was not celebrated.) All marked important transitions, and the Inca celebrated them with special feasts and ceremonies.

A baby was named on its first birthday, the date of its first ritualistic haircut. Friends and relatives were invited to a great party, where there was much drinking and dancing. After the feast, which had been specially prepared for this occasion, the oldest male relative cut a small lock of the child's hair, fingernails, and toenails, and gave the child a

Recreation

There was little time for leisure for commoners in the Inca empire. This was true for children and adults alike. The day-to-day activities required to support a family and provide service to the empire took most of their time. What free time children had was spent playing with tops, balls, and gaming pieces. Races and mock battles were held in association with the boys' puberty rite, important training to prepare them for service in the army.

Adults played games with dice, and board games with beans as counters. Exactly how the games were played is not known. Adults also gambled and sometimes bet large sums.

Music was important to the Inca, and some of the instruments they invented are still used today. In the Andes, panpipes, made of pieces of cane cut to different lengths to produce different tones, provide a breathy, mystic music some find soothing. Other instruments include simple flutes, drums, seashell trumpets, bells, rattles, and tambourines. Music was apparently provided in festivals, in war, and for *m'ita* laborers as they worked for the empire.

Two Inca noblemen carry the emperor's mummified body wrapped in a shroud in this 16th-century drawing.

name. Other relatives cut locks of hair and gave the child gifts. A permanent name was given later, at the puberty ritual.

A boy's puberty ceremony differed from that of a girl. A girl was isolated in her home, where she fasted for three days. On the fourth day, relatives came, and the girl was bathed, dressed in new clothes, and had her hair braided. Her oldest male relative gave her a permanent name and she received gifts from everyone in attendance.

The boys' coming-of-age ceremony was much more extensive. At the beginning of the rainy season, all fourteen-year-old boys went to a sacred mountain to pray. Each boy brought a llama, which was sacrificed. When the boys returned home, their relatives whipped them on the legs to make them strong and brave. At the end of the ritual, each boy received his loincloth (a symbol of manhood), weapons (usually a shield, a sling, and a mace, or club), and had his earlobes pierced.

When it came time to marry, *ayllu* leaders sometimes told young Incan men and women whom they would marry. Incan nobles could have more than one wife, but the first marriage was the only one that required a ceremony. Secondary wives were simply taken into the household.

At a person's death, life's final transition, the Inca performed special ceremonies to ensure that person a proper passage from this world to the next. The corpse was wrapped in a shroud with some possessions, including hair and nails that had been trimmed during the person's lifetime. Other possessions were burned before the body was buried.

Emperors were treated differently at death. The body was preserved, probably with herbs, and then taken high into the mountains. There, the cold, dry air helped to naturally mummify the body. Because the emperor was thought to be divine, he could not be considered dead. Instead of being buried, the mummified bodies of Incan emperors were kept in their palaces, where they were surrounded by their wealth and attended by servants and family members.

CHAPTER THREE

Science and Technology

Much of the technology associated with the Inca empire—the use of quipu (knotted strings to keep records), irrigation systems, paved roads, intricate work with gold and silver, and precise stonework—did not originate with them. Each originated with earlier civilizations from the Andes, cultures that were later conquered by the Inca. What made the Inca great was their ability to refine others' technology, to improve it, and to use it on a massive scale.

Mathematics

One skill the Inca perfected was accounting. Despite the lack of a written language, the Inca were able to keep detailed records of their population and commerce. Rather than writing down population census, crop reports, taxation records, and trading accounts, the Inca used quipus.

Quipus are cords to which are attached cotton or wool strings, sometimes hundreds of them, in various colors and lengths. Knots of various sizes were tied at irregular intervals along the strings, and the readers of the quipus could remember what the knots stood for and interpret them months or years later. In fact, the keepers of the quipus were more than accountants. They were historians

Opposite Page: Inca historians use the quipu, a knotted cord used for record keeping.

for the Inca—official "rememberers." Quipus could be used to record anything from the number of men available for *m'ita* labor in a particular month to the quantity of corn in every granary in the land.

The quipu would have been useless without a system of numbering. The Inca used a decimal system, including the concept of zero. They also developed standardized units of measurement—units of distance, weight, volume, and area. These measurements were particularly important in agriculture and architecture.

Agriculture

Terraced hillsides like this one near Cusco in Peru are still used for growing crops on the slopes of the Andes.

To take care of the food needs of the ever-expanding empire, the Inca had to reshape entire landscapes. They did this by terracing mountain-sides, straightening rivers, draining or filling marshes, and channeling water into the deserts.

A common site in the Andes today is the agricultural terrace. Because of the steepness of most of the land, it was necessary to build terraces, which resemble huge stairways, on the mountainsides. The terraces contained enough flat land to grow the amount of food needed to support the empire. The Inca built stone retaining walls along the slopes of mountains and filled the space behind them with rocks and soil, creating flat surfaces. Although this practice predated the Inca, they used the technology to its maximum potential. In all, about 2.5 million acres (1.01 million hectares) were created this way. Many Incan terraces are still in use today.

Along with terraces, irrigation systems in the form of canals and raised aqueducts (bridges that carry water over gullies) were built to bring water to crops and to the cities. The Inca also built reservoirs to store precious water for the dry season. This technology, like the building of roads and bridges, originated with earlier cultures, but the Inca perfected it.

The Inca built suspension bridges which they used to cross steep canyons.

Roads and Bridges

The Incan road system was one of the largest in the ancient world. Over 14,000 miles (23,000km) of all-weather roads crisscrossed the Inca empire. Some had been built before the existence of the Inca empire, but the Inca greatly expanded them. Most were paved with flat stones and had curbs along the sides. Since the Inca never developed the wheel, roads were usually fairly narrow, designed for foot traffic.

Mountain roads had to cross raging rivers and steep canyons in the Andes. For this, the Inca built suspension bridges. These bridges, constructed of rope, were hung from towers on either side of the canyon, with a walkway of sticks and woven grass between the ropes. Some bridges were as long as 200 feet (60m) long.

Architecture

Perhaps the greatest achievements of the Inca were in the fields of architecture, engineering, and masonry. Hundreds of Incan stone structures survive today in Peru, one of the most earthquake-prone regions of the world. Modern buildings collapse, but Incan structures remain standing.

The Inca were master engineers, as their roads and irrigation systems demonstrate, but it is in their stone buildings and walls

The Inca were masters of stonework and masonry, as shown by this Incan entranceway guarded by stone jaguars (inset).

that their skills stand out. In structures like the temple fortress Sacsahuamán, Incan stoneworkers fitted stones together weighing from 20 to 100 tons (18 to 91MT) without the use of mortar, the wheel, iron tools, or large beasts of burden.

Twenty thousand men worked thirty years to build this fortress. They used stone tools to cut the blocks, and wooden or bronze pry bars, ramps, and sheer manpower to move them. Evidence suggests they positioned one stone above another on logs to space them apart and then carved them to fit perfectly together. Some oddly shaped stones resemble pieces to a jigsaw puzzle that are fitted together with amazing precision.

Machu Picchu, Lost City of the Inca

One of the best examples of Incan architecture is the city of Machu Picchu. Remarkably well preserved since the days of the Inca empire, Machu Picchu lies along a ridge above the Urubamba River, 50 miles (80km) northwest of Cusco. This city went undiscovered until 1911, when a young American explorer, Hiram Bingham, found it. Since the Spanish did not discover this stronghold during the conquest, the only damage Bingham reported was that the thatched roofs had decayed and fallen in. Otherwise, the buildings were just as the Inca had left them.

Bingham reported stonework at Machu Picchu of the finest quality. White granite stones line a cave he believed had served as a burial place for nobility. Finely carved stones create a series of fountains running through the city. One building, thought to be a temple, rises from a rock formation that resembles the wings of a condor, a South American bird considered holy by the Inca. A rock in front of the structure is carved into the shape of the bird's head. A semicircular building nearby apparently served as a temple to the Sun god.

Metalworking

To the Inca, gold was "the sweat of the Sun," and silver was "the tears of the Moon." Most of the objects they created from these metals were destroyed during the Spanish Conquest, melted down, and shipped to Spain, but a few items escaped the greed of the conquistadores. Some members of the Spanish army saw the artistry of the Inca and wrote about what they had seen.

Most impressive to the Spaniards was the *coricancha*, or "golden enclosure," the Temple of the Sun in the center of Cusco. The chronicler Pedro Cieza de León, quoted in *Incas: Lords of Gold and Glory* by the editors of Time-Life Books, declared it "among the richest in gold and silver to be found anywhere in the world." He described how

> halfway up the wall ran a stripe of gold two hand-spans wide and four fingers thick. The gateway and doors were covered with sheets of this metal. There was an image of the sun, of great size, made of gold, beautifully wrought and set with many precious stones. There was a garden in which the earth was lumps of fine gold, and it was cunningly planted with stalks of corn that were of gold—stalk, leaves, and ears.

The Inca used the sacred intiwatana for religious ceremonies and astronomical purposes. The 6-foot stone pillar looks like a nearby mountain peak.

It features a narrow window through which rays of the sunrise on the longest day of the year enter and fall parallel to a line carved into a sacred rock.

In a place of prominence at Machu Picchu is the *intiwatana*, a 6-foot (1.8m), four-sided pillar carved from the native rock to resemble a nearby mountain peak. Like the Temple of the Sun, it apparently had astronomical uses. From its location, various land-marks surrounding the city align with the cardinal directions and the movements of the Sun and stars. Scientists believe Incan priests performed ceremonies at the *intiwatana* to honor Inti, the Sun god.

CHAPTER FOUR

Empire of the Sun

To the Inca, religion was central to life. Theirs was a complicated religion. They worshipped many deities (gods and goddesses), used myths to explain natural phenomena, and practiced complex public rituals and simple private ones to please their gods. Priests performed public ceremonies, while individuals performed private rituals such as making offerings to their gods and praying.

Major Incan Gods and Goddesses

The creator god of the Inca was Viracocha. This god created the earth, humans, and animals. The Inca believed Viracocha created men and women at Tiahuánaco, near the southern shore of Lake Titicaca, and gave them tribal customs and language. Viracocha then sent them into the earth to emerge from caves, lakes, and hills to make settlements.

After creating humankind, Viracocha supposedly came to Earth, as an old white man who carried a staff, to teach humans how to live. When he finished, he left the coast of South America near present-day Manta, Ecuador, and walked westward across the surface of the Pacific Ocean. The Inca believed he would return in times of crisis. When the Spanish arrived in the 1500s, many believed Viracocha had returned.

Inti, the Sun god, was the most important of Incan gods. Since his warmth brought life to Incan crops, he was also the god of agriculture. The Inca made offerings of guinea pigs, alpaca wool, and sometimes llamas to Inti in hopes he would provide them good harvests, long lives, and good fortune. Inti's wife was Mama-Quilla, the Moon goddess.

Opposite Page: This stone statue depicts Viracocha, the Incan creator god. Religion was an important part of Incan culture.

This ceramic vase shows Inca priests sacrificing children to the Sun god Inti.

Illapa was the god of rain and thunder. He was important because of his effect on agriculture. Illapa was usually depicted as a man in the sky who wore shiny clothing and held a war club in one hand and a sling in the other. During droughts, the Inca prayed and sometimes sacrificed llamas and humans to appease him.

The Inca explained thunder and rain with a myth associated with Illapa and his sister. His sister drew water from a heavenly river, the Milky Way, and kept it in a jug. When Illapa threw a lightning bolt, it struck the jug and made the sound of thunder. This broke the jug and caused rain to fall to Earth.

Two other goddesses, Pacha-Mama, "Earth Mother," and Mama-Cocha, goddess of the sea, were also important. Because of the earth's role in raising crops, Pacha-Mama was a special goddess for farmers. Mama-Cocha was considered the source of all water, including streams, rivers, and irrigation water. For this reason, farmers also made offerings to her.

Huacas, Amulets, and Omens

In addition to their many deities, the Inca believed that many places and objects had supernatural powers. These were called *huacas*. It is unclear, however, whether it was the locations and objects themselves that held power, or if they were just the places where spirits resided. Locations such as mountains, streams, tombs, or temples could be

Trepanning

Many Incan skeletons have been found with holes in their skulls. The Inca believed evil spirits inside a person could be released if a hole was sawed into the skull. This procedure is called trepanning. They drugged the patient with coca leaves or *chicha*, peeled back the scalp, and cut square holes into the skull

A scientist examines a trepanned skull.

with sharp stone tools to remove the bone. Some skulls have holes as large as 1 to 2 inches (2.5 to 5 cm) across. Many skulls discovered by scientists show healing around the edges of the hole, indicating that the patient survived the procedure.

huacas. Boundary markers were *huacas*, as were piles of stones, called *apachitas*, that marked mountain passes. The planet Venus was considered a *huaca*, along with anything unusual—twins, an unusual stone, a double ear of corn, even a person born feetfirst instead of headfirst.

Some *huacas* were portable. Many Inca, especially emperors, carried amulets, small objects thought to carry supernatural power. Emperor Pachacuti, for example, carried an image of Illapa, the thunder god, for protection. The Inca also believed in omens—signs or events in nature that supposedly predict the future. Evil omens foretold disasters. To the Inca, halos around the Moon, lightning that struck a holy place, earthquakes, higher than normal tides, and the appearance of comets, owls, or a sick eagle that fell from the sky could all signal bad times ahead.

Rituals

The Inca believed the correct practice of religious ritual was essential to keep their gods happy and to ward off evil spirits. Almost all rituals involved some form of sacrifice to the gods. Food, *chicha*, and coca leaves were common items to offer the *huacas.* The offerings were usually burned or poured on the ground. Animals, such as guinea pigs or llamas, were sacrificed. Each main deity required a particular color of llama for its sacrifice—brown for Viracocha, white for Inti, and mixed color for Illapa.

Ceremonies in times of natural disaster, war, or at the coronation of a new emperor required human sacrifice—always children between the ages of ten and fifteen. This ritual was called *capacocha.* These children had to be physically perfect. The Inca believed children were more pure than adults and the most precious thing that could be offered to the gods. To be selected for sacrifice was considered a great

honor, even by those individuals chosen from conquered peoples. Following a specially prepared feast, the victim was either strangled, had his or her throat cut, or had his or her heart cut out and offered to the deity. Victims sacrificed to mountain *huacas* were often drugged before being killed and then mummified.

Some Incan rituals were performed annually. The three most important were Capac Raymi in December, Aymoray in May, and Inti Raymi in June. Capac Raymi celebrated the beginning of the rainy season. This was the time of male puberty rituals. Aymoray celebrated the corn harvest. Inti Raymi was the most important of many festivals that honored the Sun god Inti. The entire festival was conducted on a hill near Cusco, and only Incan males of royal blood were allowed to attend. This event involved the sacrifice of hundreds of llamas, not only to Inti but also to Viracocha and Illapa.

In addition to ceremonies associated with the calendar or for the good of the empire, there were ceremonies to cure disease or to predict the future. The Inca did not believe illness was the result of natural causes, but that supernatural forces brought it about. For that reason, priests tried to cure disease by appeasing whatever spirit had caused the illness. This usually involved some sort of sacrifice, the application of plants thought to have magical powers, or a process called trepanning, in which holes were cut into people's skulls to cure illnesses or to release evil spirits.

Today, millions of people live in the lands of the former Inca empire—from Ecuador in the north to Chile and Argentina in the south. Many are descendants of the peoples of *Tahuantinsuyu*, the Land of the Four Quarters, either of the Inca themselves or of those they conquered. Five-sixths of the people in Peru, Ecuador, and Bolivia, for example, still speak Quechua, the language of the Inca. Many still see their world as being divided into four quarters.

Much of the Inca's legacy remains in rural regions of western South America—agricultural terraces and irrigation systems, massive stone structures, the *ayllu* system of community organization, and their vast system of roads. Elements of Inca religion are still evident in some of the region's Catholic rituals. Today, there is a reawakening of interest and pride in Inca heritage. Inca-built waterworks and terraces are being reclaimed. Foods developed by the Inca appear on grocery shelves around the world. Peruvian schoolchildren recite the names of Inca rulers, names that evoke images of a creative people, of an orderly and progressive empire, and of remarkable achievements.

Notes

Chapter 1: Incan Government and Society

    1. Quoted in Ron Fisher, et al., *Builders of the Ancient World: Marvels of Engineering.* Washington, DC: National Geographic Society, 1986, p. 114.

Chapter 2: Daily Life

    2. Quoted in Joseph J. Thorndike Jr., ed., *Discovery of Lost Worlds.* New York: American Heritage, 1979, p. 255.

Glossary

alpaca: One of the domesticated South American members of the camel family, bred for its fine wool.

apu: The person in charge of one of the quarters of the Inca empire.

ayllu: The basic unit of Incan society.

chicha: Beer, usually made of corn, but other grains or fruit could be used.

coca: A domesticated plant grown for its leaves, which are chewed as a stimulant to reduce feelings of fatigue, hunger, or thirst; used to make cocaine.

conquistador: The Spanish word for conqueror; a Spanish soldier and adventurer, part of the Spanish expedition to the New World in the 1500s.

earplugs: Metal or wooden disks inserted into holes in the earlobes.

huaca: A place or object with supernatural powers.

llama: One of the domesticated South American members of the camel family, bred as a beast of burden.

m'ita **labor:** The Incan labor tax; time required of all conquered people to work in some capacity for the empire.

Quechua: The language of the Inca; still spoken by 3 million people in Peru, Ecuador, and Bolivia.

quipu: A knotted cord device that was used in Incan accounting.

terrace: An artificially leveled field used to increase agricultural land in steeply sloping areas.

thatch: A roof covering made from straw, grass, or reeds.

tunic: A loose, sleeveless garment, similar to a poncho.

For More Information

Books

Elizabeth Baquedano, *Eyewitness: Aztec, Inca, and Maya.* New York: DK, July 2000.

Arlette N. Braman, *The Inca: Activities and Crafts from a Mysterious Land.* Hoboken, NJ: Wiley, 2003.

Kathryn Hinds, *The Incas.* Tarrytown, NY: Marshall Cavendish, 1998.

Fiona MacDonald, *Inca Town.* New York: Scholastic Library, 1999.

Elizabeth Mann, *Machu Picchu: The Story of the Amazing Inkas and Their City in the Clouds.* New York: Mikaya, April 2000.

Neil Morris, *Everyday Life of the Aztecs, Inca, and Maya.* Mankato, MN: Smart Apple Media, 2004.

Sue Nicholson, *Aztecs and Incas: A Guide to the Pre-Colonized Americas in 1504.* Boston: Houghton Mifflin, 2000.

Rosemary Rees, *Incas.* Portsmouth, NH: Heinemann Library, 2001.

Duncan Scheff, *Incas.* Chicago: Raintree, 2002.

Jane Shuter, *Incas.* Portsmouth, NH: Heinemann Library, 2002.

Web Sites

Ancient Incas (www.awesomelibrary.org/Classroom/Social_Studies/Ancient_Civilizations/ Ancient_Incas.html). Produced by Awesome Library, an award-winning database created by R. Jerry Adams, with numerous links to Inca information sites, including sites constructed by students.

Incas & Conquistadors (www.incaconquest.com). An excellent site created by amateur historian David Bailey, with links and detailed information about the history of the Inca and their empire.

Machu Picchu, a Photo Gallery(www.jqjacobs.net/andes/machu.html). A photo gallery of Machu Picchu, lost city of the Inca, with links to other photo sites, including one on Sacsahuamán. Shows details of Incan stonework. Produced by professional photographer James Q. Jacobs.

The Topic: Incas (www.42explore2.com/inca.htm). Part of the 42explore database, a thematic Web site for teachers and students. An excellent Web site with numerous links for further study about all aspects of the Inca and their history and culture. Includes Web pages for kids, produced by kids.

Index

Picture Credits

About the Authors

Charles George and his wife Linda have written more than fifty nonfiction books for children and teens. Their books include *Texas, The Sioux, The Comanche, The Holocaust, Plate Tectonics*, and *Uranus* for KidHaven Press, and *The Maya*, part of the Life During the Great Civilizations series, for Blackbirch Press. They both taught in Texas public schools before "retiring" to write full time. Charles taught secondary history and Spanish, and Linda taught in the elementary grades. They live in the mountains of New Mexico.